D1607231

SOMERSET CO. LIBRARY
BRIDGEWATER, N.J. 08807

Weird America!

AMERICA'S ODDEST
MUSEUMS

By M. H. Seeley

Gareth Stevens
PUBLISHING

Somerset Co. Library
Bridgewater, NJ 08807

Please visit our website, www.garethstevens.com. For a free color catalog of all our high-quality books, call toll free 1-800-542-2595 or fax 1-877-542-2596.

Library of Congress Cataloging-in-Publication Data

Names: Seeley, M. H., author.
Title: America's oddest museums / M.H. Seeley.
Description: New York : Gareth Stevens Publishing, 2017. | Series: Weird America | Includes index.
Identifiers: LCCN 2016039993| ISBN 9781482457599 (pbk. book) | ISBN 9781482457605 (6 pack) | ISBN 9781482457612 (library bound book)
Subjects: LCSH: Museums–United States. | Curiosities and wonders–United States.
Classification: LCC E151 .S4535 2017 | DDC 069.0973–dc23
LC record available at https://lccn.loc.gov/2016039993

First Edition

Published in 2017 by
Gareth Stevens Publishing
111 East 14th Street, Suite 349
New York, NY 10003

Copyright © 2017 Gareth Stevens Publishing

Designer: Sarah Liddell
Editor: Ryan Nagelhout

Photo credits: Cover, p. 1 (arrow) Mascha Tace/Shutterstock.com; cover, pp. 1 (main), 21 Darb02/
Wikimedia Commons; sidebar used throughout zayats-and-zayats/Shutterstock.com; brick background texture used
throughout multipear/Shutterstock.com; screen texture used throughout donatas1205/Shutterstock.com;
p. 5 Jovianeye/Wikimedia Commons; p. 7 Al Freni/Contributor/The LIFE Images Collection/Getty Images;
p. 9 Keystone/Stringer/Hulton Archive/Getty Images; p. 11 Sacramento Bee/Contributor/Tribune News Service/
Getty Images; p. 12 Ovidiu Hrubaru/Shutterstock.com; p. 13 Perry Riddle/Contributor/Los Angeles Times/
Getty Images; p. 15 Infrogmation/Wikimedia Commons; p. 17 Margo Harrison/Shutterstock.com; p. 18 ANCH/
Shutterstock.com; p. 19 Michael Ochs Archives/Stringer/Michael Ochs Archives/Getty Images; p. 20 abimages/
Shutterstock.com; p. 23 (frames) Sabelskaya/Shutterstock.com; p. 23 (mobile museums) Aelffin/Wikimedia Commons;
p. 24 vdimage/Shutterstock.com; p. 25 Gaylon Wampler/Getty Images p. 27 Nv8200pa/Wikimedia Commons;
p. 29 We hope/Wikimedia Commons

All rights reserved. No part of this book may be reproduced in any form without permission in writing from
the publisher, except by a reviewer.

Printed in the United States of America

CPSIA compliance information: Batch #CW17GS: For further information contact Gareth Stevens, New York, New York at 1-800-542-2595.

CONTENTS

Words in the glossary appear in **bold** type the first time they are used in the text.

THE MET AND MORE

The Metropolitan Museum of Art in New York City is one of the world's most famous museums. But America is full of smaller museums **dedicated** to local, personal, and sometimes just plain weird things. Every museum, and every museum **curator**, has their own ideas of what's worth remembering.

You might think of museums as huge buildings filled with art or ancient objects, but most are less fancy. Whether it's a town's local history, a collection of unique—or special—objects, or a snapshot of a historical moment, museums are places where people can connect with the past, sometimes in weird and wonderful ways.

America's Oldest Museums

Founded in 1799, the oldest museum in America that's still open is the Peabody Essex Museum in Salem, Massachusetts. The second oldest is the Charleston Museum, which was founded in South Carolina in 1773, but didn't open to the public until 1824. The Charleston Museum is also famous for hiring America's first female art museum director, Laura Bragg, in 1920.

The Field Museum, Chicago's natural history museum, is home to the world's most complete Tyrannosaurus rex fossil, named Sue. Sue is about 67 million years old!

THE HORSE

WAKING THE T REX

THE STORY OF SUE IN 3-D

NOT FOR SALE ANYWHERE

The Museum of Failed Products isn't just weird—it's huge! Dedicated to bad products of every kind, this museum in Ann Arbor, Michigan, is home to thousands of ideas and inventions that went nowhere.

These ideas failed for all kinds of reasons. Some products—such as fortune cookies for dogs called Fortune Snookies—were too weird for people to buy. Others were inventions no one wanted, such as shampoo made out of yogurt. Many products just never worked correctly, such as self-cooking soup cans that often exploded! We're probably better off without most of these products—yogurt shampoo sounds pretty gross!

If at First You Don't Succeed

Many of the objects in the Museum of Failed Products come from big companies you might recognize: Coca-Cola, Pepsi, or Colgate. Even successful companies fail sometimes and have to try something new. So remember: If at first you don't succeed, try again! Who knows, your idea might be the next big thing!

New Coke definitely belongs
in the Museum of Failed Products,
which is actually called Gfk Custom
Research North America. New Coke
debuted in 1985 as a change in flavor
of Coca Cola. Many people hated it!

7

BIGFOOTS AND MONSTERS

The word "cryptozoology" means the "study of hidden animals," but in practice, it often means **investigations** into what we might call monsters! Bigfoot, the Loch Ness monster, and the Abominable Snowman are all subjects of interest to cryptozoologists, who spend their lives trying to prove these cryptids, or monsters, exist.

The International Cryptozoology Museum in Portland, Maine, claims to be the only museum of its kind. It houses **artifacts**, re-creations of cryptids, and other objects as proof of these animals' existence. Some of the things on display include hair samples claimed to be from a Yeti, models of Bigfoot and a baby Bigfoot, and a full Lake Monster exhibit.

American Monsters

America is known for having some pretty weird monster legends. The hodag from Wisconsin is said to have horns and huge teeth, as well as "the head of a frog, the face of an elephant, the back of a dinosaur, and a long tail with spears at the end."

8

This famed picture of "Nessie," the Loch Ness monster, was exposed as a fake when one of the men who took it confessed that it had been staged.

9

MUSEUM OF DEATH

If you want to visit the world's grimmest museum, you have two choices: Hollywood, California, and New Orleans, Louisiana. The Museum of Death started in San Diego, in a building once owned by famous Wild West sheriff Wyatt Earp. It later moved to Hollywood and opened a second location in New Orleans. Its collections mostly center on **gruesome** murders, **executions**, and **autopsies**, with the aim of teaching people about death in our society.

If you can't make it out to California or Louisiana, the museum's owners also got their own TV show where they showed off objects on display at the museum!

Death-Dealer Wyatt Earp

Wyatt Earp dealt his fair share of death during his days as a lawman in the Wild West. Earp took part in one of America's most famous gunfights: the shootout at OK Corral, when Earp and his crew faced off against a gang of cowboy criminals.

The Museum of Death's Hollywood location has a special California Death Room featuring murderers like Charles Manson and other famous crimes from the state like the Black Dahlia murder.

11

THE BANANA MUSEUM

There are over 20,000 banana-related items in California's International Banana Museum. What started as a personal hobby grew into a world-record–setting collection for museum founder Ken Bannister. Items on display include banana phones, clocks, coloring books, toys, record players, costumes, golf clubs, stuffed animals, and even ceiling fans!

By donating a banana item to the museum, you can become a Banana Club member, choose your own Banana Club nickname, and win "banana merit" points. Earn enough points, and you could get a degree in "Bananistry." Famous Banana Club members include some celebrities and even former US president Ronald Reagan!

That's Bananas!

Bananas are a weird fruit. For example, did you know most banana plants are clones of a single plant in Southeast Asia? Or did you know they're naturally **radioactive**? Bananas were once so popular in the United States that when new immigrants arrived at Ellis Island, they were handed a banana as a welcome gift!

The Banana Museum is filled with strange and unusual banana-themed objects, including a banana covered with gold **sequins** and a banana made out of the costly green stone called jade. That's bananas!

13

ABITA MYSTERY HOUSE

The Abita Mystery House, also known as the UCM Museum, may be Louisiana's strangest museum. Located in Abita Springs, its collection grew out of the idea that one person's trash is another person's treasure. Artist and inventor John Preble used only objects he found or recycled to create a whole miniature world that includes a Mardi Gras parade, a haunted plantation, and a rhythm-and-blues dance hall.

There are also the sculptures of Buford, a 26-foot (8 m) "bassigator" (a mix of a bass fish and alligator) and Darrel, the "dogigator" (a mix of a dog and alligator). Visitors enter the museum through an old gas station!

That's All, Folks!

Preble specialized in folk art. "Folk" means "people," and folk art centers on themes relating to specific groups. Since all groups have their own traditions, folk art is very **diverse** and hard to describe. But a lot of folk art serves a purpose and is colorful, like a quilt.

It may not look like much,
but inside this building is
an entire tiny world.

UCM MUSEUM
ABITA SPRIN

MYSTERY HOUSE

OPEN
10-5
COLD
DRINKS

15

O'FALLON HISTORICAL MUSEUM

Most museums in this book have a collection of things or focus on a certain subject. But the O'Fallon Historical Museum takes this another step further by having one huge main attraction: Steer Montana, the largest steer that ever lived.

You can also find true-to-life re-creations of other life in Montana during the early 1900s, but the **taxidermy** display of Steer Montana is by far the most popular. The huge, record-setting bull stands nearly 6 feet (1.8 m) tall, 10 feet (3 m) long, and 9 feet (2.7 m) around his middle and weighs nearly 4,000 pounds (1,814 kg)!

Steer Wrestling

It doesn't get much more "American West" than steer wrestling at the rodeo. In this event, a cowboy chases a steer on horseback. Then he jumps from the horse onto a 600–pound (272 kg) steer and wrestles it to the ground. It's the quickest event in rodeo, but also one of the most dangerous.

Steer wrestling, or bulldogging, is a popular event at rodeos—can you imagine wrestling a steer as big as Steer Montana?

THE SARDINE MUSEUM

There's just one thing on the table at the Maine Sardine Museum. Can you guess what it is? That's right: sardines, sardines, sardines! Fishing and canning sardines were important parts of Maine's economy from the 1870s until the early 2000s, and this museum puts on display not just the details of the business, but also the lives of the people who kept it going.

Displays include a can exhibit showing more than 100 different types of sardine cans. The museum also features some fishing tools, a can-sealing machine, and a wall of scissors used by real women who worked in factories packing sardines into cans.

They don't look very tasty, but canned sardines would be very useful if the world were to end: If unopened, they'll stay safe to eat for up to 5 years!

Small Fish, Big Nutrients

Sardines may be small fish, but they pack a big punch! Just one can of sardines is loaded with **omega-3 fatty acids**, calcium, and almost all the B vitamins you need. They also have almost no mercury, which is often found in fish and can make humans very sick. Sardines make for a great snack!

HOW MUCH SPAM? A LOT!

Probably the most famous canned meat is Spam, a mix of pork and spices. The "mystery meat" was invented by the Hormel Corporation and gained popularity during World War II, when it was fed to soldiers who hated it. Hormel even kept a file of soldiers' hate mail!

But not everyone hated it—Spam is popular in many places around the world, including Hawaii. In fact, when Hormel first opened the Spam museum in 1991 in Austin, Minnesota, it was quickly overwhelmed by visitors. Hormel opened a large, new museum in 2002, then moved to a newer location in 2016. You can see Spam through the years and even work in a mock Spam assembly line!

The original Spam museum was too small to manage the high level of interest, so the Hormel Corporation had a new building constructed just for Spam exhibits.

What Makes the Meat a Mystery?

Meat "products" like Spam are ground or processed meats that don't come from a specific source. They're generally a mix of meat and other ingredients. Sometimes those "other ingredients" are pretty gross—but sometimes they're simply added flavor, like spices. Many people are fine with not knowing exactly what's in Spam—as long as it tastes good!

SPAM Brand

BROKEN HEARTS ON DISPLAY

It's hard to say goodbye to people we love. The Museum of Broken Relationships originally opened in Croatia, but has a US branch in Los Angeles, California. The museum is a memorial to the objects that remind someone of their lost love: love notes, gifts, and even common household items.

Each exhibit comes with a little story about the object, written by the person who gave the object to the museum. The story tells what happened, how it got there, and why it represents the relationship. The exhibits are designed to offer people a way to celebrate, mourn, and learn from their experiences with love and loss.

Mobile Museums

For less populated communities, mobile museums that don't charge an entrance fee are a way to bring exhibits to people. Some museums don't even have a permanent, or long-lasting, building and spend all their time on the road! One sweet example was an ice cream museum that popped up in New York City in 2016. Maybe it'll visit a town near you someday!

MUSEUMS ON THE MOVE

Discovering
the Universe
Movable Museum

Structures
& Culture
Movable Museum

Paleontology
of Dinosaurs
Movable Museum

23

BARNEY SMITH'S TOILET SEAT ART MUSEUM

It's important to do what you love, and Barney Smith loves what he does. A retired master plumber, Smith's artwork began as a hobby in his garage. He began decorating old toilet seats with paint and trinkets. Soon, the collection grew so large that he got enough publicity to open his garage to the public as the Toilet Seat Art Museum.

There's no entry fee, but Smith encourages visitors to bring along a toilet seat that he can use in his next project. He'll even carve your name on it, so future visitors will know who gave each seat!

Barney Smith still runs the Toilet Seat Art Museum out of his garage in San Antonio, Texas.

Art in Odd Places

The US-based group Art in Odd Places takes the idea of finding art in unexpected places to the next level, turning regular city streets, parks, and neighborhoods into art displays for people who wouldn't usually go to a museum.

MUSEUM OF THE WEIRD

What's weirder than a museum dedicated to the weird? Austin, Texas, is home to what's been called America's strangest attraction, a museum that has exhibits focusing on the spooky, the unexplained, and the just plain bizarre. The museum is not only filled with weird objects and **relics**, but also has daily sideshows where people with unique talents can show off their weird abilities.

Probably the most popular attraction of the Museum of the Weird is the Minnesota Iceman, which displays a humanlike creature frozen in a block of ice. Some think this creature is a Bigfoot, others think he's an early human, and some say he's a fake!

Get Your Freak On

Sideshows are any secondary show at a larger attraction, usually a circus or carnival. They're often showcases for strange performances or talents, such as sword swallowing, fire eating, knife throwing, and lying on a bed of nails. These skills take a lot of training and maybe a bit of courage!

The Museum of the Weird isn't particularly large, but it's full of weird and wonderful displays.

CABINET of CURIOSITIES

Sixth Street, Austin, TX

MUSEUM OF THE WEIRD

COLLECTION of ODDITIES

GIFTS   NTIQUES   SOUVE IRS   HANDMADES

MUSEUM OF THE WEIRD

THE DUMMY GRAVEYARD

Ventriloquism (vehn-TRIH-luh-kwih-zuhm) is the art of speaking in such a way that the sound seems to come from somewhere or someone else—often a dummy sitting on the ventriloquist's lap. The Ventriloquist Museum in Fort Mitchell, Kentucky, is the only museum in the world dedicated to this type of stage act, which was hugely popular in the days before television and radio.

These sometimes creepy-looking ventriloquist dummies come in many shapes and sizes. Today, the museum has built its collection from things donated, or given, by the families of ventriloquists after they've passed away, leading some to call this museum the "ventriloquist dummy graveyard."

Don't Be a Dummy!

Ventriloquist dummies, puppets, and marionettes often all get lumped in together, but each type is different. A marionette is controlled by strings, while a ventriloquist dummy is controlled through a hole in its back where the ventriloquist's hand goes. Puppets, meanwhile, are controlled in many different ways and can come in any size.

Ventriloquist dummies were made with strong features so that people in the back of theaters could see them—but it made the dolls hard to film without looking creepy.

GLOSSARY

artifact: an object that has been made by an intelligent creature and is not simply a product of nature

autopsy: the act of examining a dead body to find the cause of death

curator: a person in charge of museum exhibits

dedicate: to set something apart for a certain purpose

diverse: having a lot of different forms or qualities

execution: death as a punishment, usually by a government

gruesome: causing horror

investigation: the act of looking into a crime or mystery in order to figure out what happened

omega-3 fatty acid: a kind of fat that helps your body stay healthy

radioactive: putting out harmful energy in the form of tiny particles

relic: an object held in regard because of its possible ties to someone

sequin: a small, shiny piece of plastic or metal often used on clothes

taxidermy: the art of preserving a dead animal by stuffing the skin or mounting it over a wood or plaster model

FOR MORE INFORMATION

BOOKS

Hartland, Jessie. *How the Sphinx Got to the Museum.* Maplewood, NJ: Blue Apple Books, 2010.

Mark, Jan. *The Museum Book: A Guide to Strange and Wonderful Collections.* Cambridge, MA: Candlewick Press, 2007.

WEBSITES

Atlas Obscura
atlasobscura.com
Atlas Obscura is full of the world's most interesting, bizarre, and unusual places. They even have a whole museum category!

Roadside America
roadsideamerica.com
Visit this site to learn all about America's oddest offbeat attractions.

Publisher's note to educators and parents: Our editors have carefully reviewed these websites to ensure that they are suitable for students. Many websites change frequently, however, and we cannot guarantee that a site's future contents will continue to meet our high standards of quality and educational value. Be advised that students should be closely supervised whenever they access the Internet.

INDEX

J 069.09 SEE

Seeley, M. H.,

America's oddest museums

MAR 3 0 2017